Topics in Context

Context

Glimpses of the
English-Speaking World

Themenheft

Cornelsen

Context

Glimpses of the English-Speaking World

Im Auftrag des Verlages herausgegeben von
Dr. Annette Leithner-Brauns, Dresden

Erarbeitet von
Martina Baasner, Berlin; Irene Bartscherer, Bonn;
Lisa Braun, Meppen; Dr. Sabine Buchholz, Hürth; Dr. Wiebke
Bettina Dietrich, Göttingen; Sylvia Loh, Esslingen; Benjamin
Lorenz, Bensheim; Dr. Paul Maloney, Hildesheim; Dr. Pascal
Ohlmann, Tholey; Birgit Ohmsieder, Berlin; Dr. Andreas
Sedlatschek, Esslingen; Veronika Walther, Rudolstadt

In Zusammenarbeit mit der Englischredaktion
Dr. Marion Kiffe (Koordinierende Redakteurin), Dr. Christiane
Kallenbach (Projektleitung), Aryane Beaudoin, Dr. Jan
Dreßler, Hartmut Tschepe, Dr. Christian von Raumer, Freya
Wurm *unter Mitwirkung von* Janan Barksdale, Irja Fröhling,
Katrin Gütermann, Anne Müller, Neil Porter, Evelyn Sternad,
Mai Weber

Beratende Mitwirkung
Ramin Azadian, Berlin; Heiko Benzin, Neustrelitz;
Sabine Otto, Halle (Saale)

Layoutkonzept
Klein & Halm, Berlin

Layout und technische Umsetzung
Straive
designcollective, Berlin

Umschlaggestaltung
Rosendahl, Berlin

Lizenzmanagement
Britta Bensmann

Weitere Bestandteile des Lehrwerks

- *Schulbuch* (print und als E-Book)
- *E-Books* (in zwei Varianten: 1. alle *Topics in Context* bzw. 2. Schulbuch und *Topics in Context*)
- *Lehrkräftefassung des Schulbuchs* (im Unterrichtsmanager)
- *Handreichungen für den Unterricht* (print und im Unterrichtsmanager)
- *Workbook* (print)
- *Unterrichtsmanager*
- *Vorschläge zur Leistungsmessung* (digital)
- *Cornelsen Lernen App*

www.cornelsen.de

Die Webseiten Dritter, deren Internetadressen in diesem Lehrwerk angegeben sind,
wurden vor Drucklegung sorgfältig geprüft. Der Verlag übernimmt keine Gewähr für
die Aktualität und den Inhalt dieser Seiten oder solcher, die mit ihnen verlinkt sind.

1. Auflage, 2. Druck 2023

Alle Drucke dieser Auflage sind inhaltlich unverändert und können im Unterricht nebeneinander verwendet werden.

© 2022 Cornelsen Verlag GmbH, Berlin

Druck: AZ Druck und Datentechnik GmbH, Kempten

ISBN 978-3-06-035793-2

PEFC-zertifiziert
Dieses Produkt
stammt aus
nachhaltig
bewirtschafteten
Wäldern und
kontrollierten Quellen
PEFC/04-31-2262 www.pefc.de

Title	Topic	Text type / media	Skills	Page
Lead-in				4
Words in Context: Traces of British colonialism		Informative text		6
Text 1: Does Britain need a museum of colonialism? *Alison Flood*	Postcolonialism: between tradition and change	Newspaper article Video ▶	Speaking Viewing	8
Info box: The British Empire		Informative text		10
Text 2: Germany's colonial legacy	Postcolonialism: Living together	Video ▶	Viewing Intercultural communication	11
Info box: German colonialism		Informative text		11
Text 3: The Commonwealth – family or foe?	The Commonwealth: contemporary implications	Video ▶	Viewing Analysing videos Writing	12
Info box: The Commonwealth		Informative text		12
Text 4: Welcome to Nigeria! **Art in Context**	Nigeria: an emerging post-colonial state Nigerian identity	Pictures Infographic Video ▶	Viewing Analysing videos Intercultural communication	13
Text 5: My vision of Nigeria *Aisha Yesufu*	Reality of life vs. dream of life	Essay	Analysing non-fiction Speaking	14
Info box: Aisha Yesufu		Informative text		14
Text 6: Welcome to Singapore! 'Bumboat cruise on the Singapore River' *Miriam Wei Wei Lo*	Singapore: a multi-faceted city state	Poem	Intercultural communication Creative writing	17
Info box: Singapore		Informative text		17
Text 7: Smart Nation Singapur – die digitale Stadt *Christoph Hein*	Singapore: a modern post-colonial state	Newspaper article	Mediating	20
Text 8: Forty shades of green *Johnny Cash*	Images of Ireland	Song lyrics	Speaking	22
Info box: Irish protest songs		Informative text		24
Text 9: Democratic disruption *Bill Rolston*	Ireland: a divided nation	Online article	Analysing non-fiction Writing	24
Info box: Irish president Michael D. Higgins		Informative text		27
Chapter Task: A time capsule				27
Support and Partner B				28
Abbreviations				30
Acknowledgements				31

Glimpses of the English-Speaking World

woman wearing a cap like that worn by freed Roman slaves, which became a symbol of liberty during the French revolution

Britannia, *personification of Britain, modelled after a female Greco-Roman warrior

the Titan Atlas, from Greek mythology, carrying the world, wearing a sash reading 'human labour'

▶ Getting started

Annotations

box 3 **sash** long piece of cloth worn over one shoulder

▶ SF 22: Analysing visuals, Student's book p. 292

▶ More info

1 With a partner, recollect what you know about the British Empire.

2 Look at the map on the opposite page. Point out what it tells you about
- the size and the infrastructure of the British Empire in 1886
- Britain's view of itself as a colonial power and of the colonized people and territories.

Pay special attention to the animals and to how the people are dressed.

3 British artist and illustrator Walter Crane, a passionate socialist, included several details in the map to express his political convictions. Study the enlarged details and explain his hidden messages.

4 In this chapter you will learn about three English-speaking countries that were once part of the British Empire: Nigeria, Singapore and Ireland. Study the Chapter map, then discuss how Britain and its former colonies might still be affected by their colonial past today.

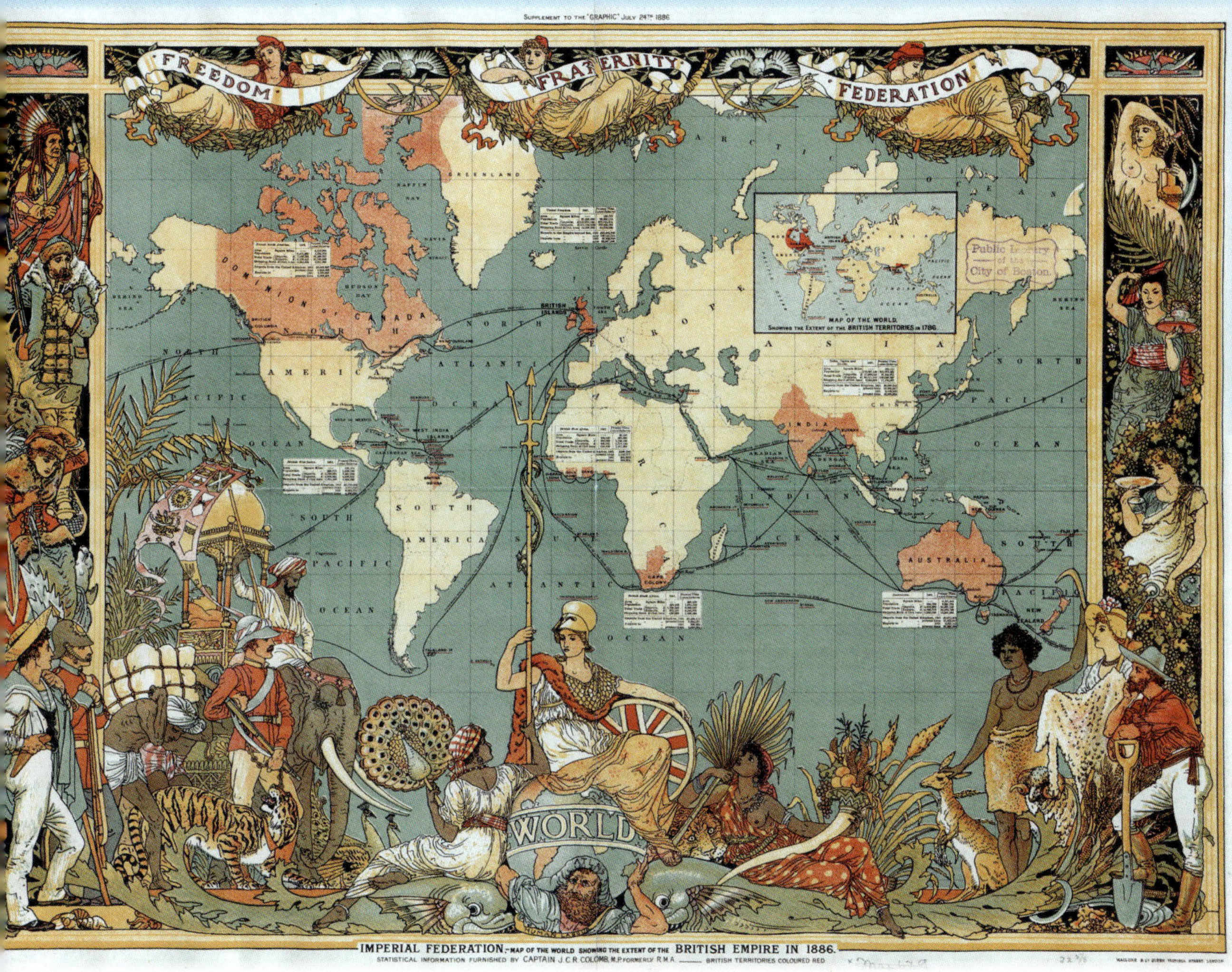

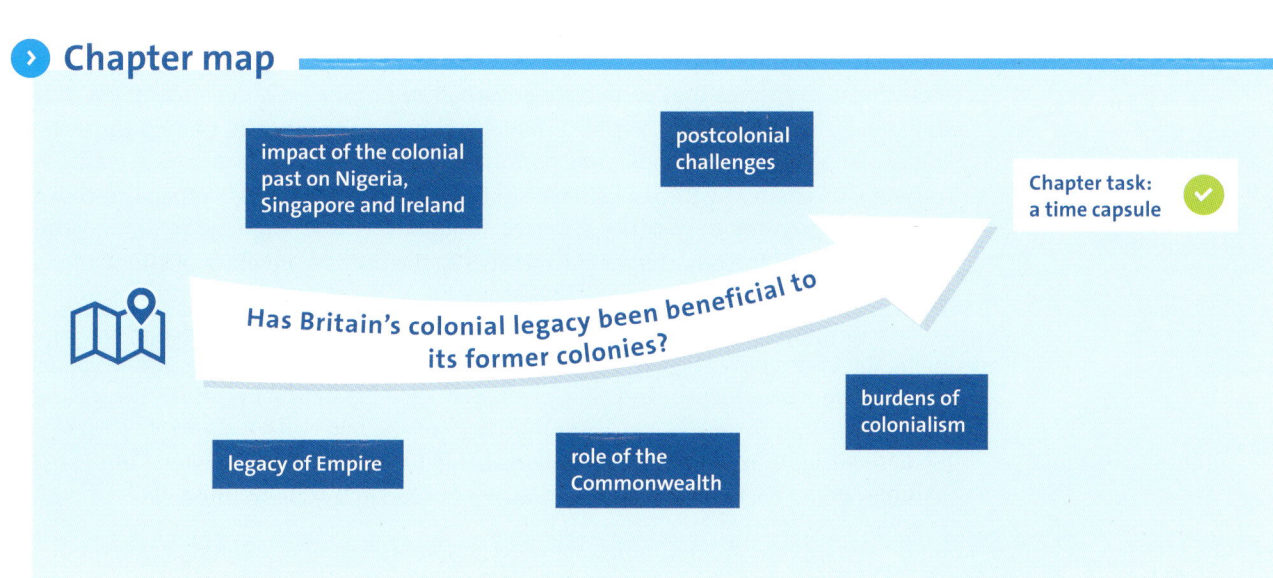

SUPPLEMENT TO THE 'GRAPHIC' JULY 24TH 1886
FREEDOM
FRATERNITY
FEDERATION
WORLD
IMPERIAL FEDERATION, MAP OF THE WORLD SHOWING THE EXTENT OF THE BRITISH EMPIRE IN 1886.
STATISTICAL INFORMATION FURNISHED BY CAPTAIN J.C.R. COLOMB, M.P. FORMERLY R.M.A. — BRITISH TERRITORIES COLOURED RED

Chapter map

- impact of the colonial past on Nigeria, Singapore and Ireland
- postcolonial challenges
- Chapter task: a time capsule

Has Britain's colonial legacy been beneficial to its former colonies?

- legacy of Empire
- role of the Commonwealth
- burdens of colonialism

🔊 **Traces of British colonialism**

▶ More language 🔖

From Empire to independence
The British Empire has had a lasting impact on Britain and the territories it once ruled. At its height, at the beginning of the 20th century, the British Empire controlled one fourth of the land surface of the globe and was home to more than 400 million people. In the decades that followed, many of them began to contest British domination and to push for independence and national sovereignty. For many territories, decolonization, i. e. gaining independence from British rule, was a long and demanding process. Colonial rule was exploitative and the newly independent countries had to deal with its consequences. In some of the new nations, the territorial boundaries and divide-and-rule strategies that were a legacy of the colonial era led to ethnic conflicts, power struggles and sometimes even civil wars.

Glimpses of the English-speaking world: Nigeria, Singapore and Ireland
The differing colonial experiences and postcolonial settings impacted the process of nation building. While some countries saw the rise of authoritarian regimes and dictatorships, others were more successful in defining their national identities and establishing stable political systems.
Nigeria, for example, which is Africa's most populous country, has been plagued by ethnic rivalries, patriarchal structures, poverty and corruption since it became independent in 1960, but it has also experienced an unprecedented economic boom which has earned the country the nickname 'giant of Africa.'
Singapore, a comparatively small city state in South-East Asia, has developed into one of the wealthiest nations on earth since it gained independence in 1965. While Singapore has assumed global leadership in areas such as education and sustainable development, its government has also been criticized for being authoritarian and curtailing citizens' freedoms.
Ireland was Britain's first colony in Europe. For centuries, the Irish resisted British oppression, and the oftentimes violent struggle for independence has left deep marks in the Irish national consciousness. After the Irish War of Independence (1919–1921), the island was divided, which has haunted Irish and British politics and societies ever since.

The legacies of the Empire
Today most territories that were once governed by Britain are independent, yet they still show visible traces of British influence in language, politics and culture. The English language, for example, has become the world's lingua franca, not least because it was spread by British colonialism. Nowadays English holds official status in numerous postcolonial societies where it functions as the language of administration, parliament, the law, the media and also as the primary medium of education in schools and universities.
Several former colonies also adopted the British parliamentary system, and many joined the Commonwealth of Nations, which was founded in 1931 to promote values such as democracy, justice, and peace and to foster cooperation in culture, sports and economy.
Despite these efforts, it must be acknowledged that imperial mindsets and racist attitudes going back to colonial times have prevailed in the UK to this day.

Line numbers: 5, 15, 20, 25, 30, 35, 40

1 Words words words

a Read the text and note down
- two expressions related to the British Empire
- two adjectives characterizing colonial rule
- two expressions that describe the legacies of the British Empire
- five expressions that reflect the main topics in the text.

b Paraphrase the following expressions:
British rule • decolonization • nation building • postcolonial settings.

c Use the terms above to summarize the text.

2 Clustering and brainstorming

a Cluster words and phrases from the text into the following groups:
British Empire, decolonization, independence and *the legacies of Empire.*

b Work with a partner and discuss which colonial legacies you consider positive and which ones negative. Together brainstorm more legacies of the Empire and add them to your cluster.

3 Chunk it!

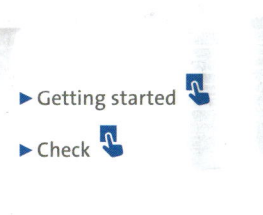

► Getting started

► Check

a Match the words on the left to those on the right to form meaningful
*collocations.

assume • curtail • establish • face • gain • leave • resist • populous • postcolonial • promote • show • push for • sustainable

a stable political system • civil war • corruption • country • deep marks • development • ethnic conflicts • experience • freedom • leadership • independence • national identity • oppression • societies • values • visible traces

b Choose either Nigeria, Singapore or Ireland and write five sentences about its development from colony to independent nation. Draw on your own knowledge or do some quick research. Use at least five collocations from **a**.

c Compare sentences with a partner and add some of your partner's information to your sentences.

4 Practice

With a partner, discuss what aspects of the British legacy might be considered a benefit for its former colonies and which aspects a disadvantage? Write a short statement to be presented in class. Use words and phrases from the text and the exercises above.

▶ More info

Does Britain need a museum of colonialism?   Alison Flood

In recent years, statues and other memorials commemorating slave traders and coloni-alists have been taken down or will be removed across the United Kingdom in response to campaigns calling for acknowledgement of Britain's colonial past and its role in the slave trade.

- Do you think it is a good idea to remove historical statues depicting controversial figures such as slave traders? What should the future of such statues be? Share your opinions in class, then read the article below that presents different opinions on the issue.

Britain should set up a 'museum of colonialism' where children will be able to learn about 'the really terrible things that happened in our past', the historian William Dalrymple has said.

Dalrymple, speaking in the final debate at the Jaipur literature festival (JLF) on
5 whether statues in Britain of former imperial heroes who would now be seen as war criminals should be placed in a museum of colonialism, or stay where they are, said that while he 'certainly wouldn't want to see most of the nation's statues torn down', people 'have to use discrimination'. The debate followed the toppling of the statue of the slaver Edward Colston in Bristol in June. [...]

10 'It's not a matter of being woke or a matter of being fashionable or trendy but it's being realistic about some of the really terrible things that happened in our past and teaching them to our children. If we put them in a museum of colonialism, this is an opportunity to teach, because we can set up a museum, which will do what at the moment the curriculum fails to do.' [...]

15 Dalrymple said that the history curriculum for British school children sees them move 'from Henry VIII to Wilberforce and the impression they get is that the British empire was always about liberating slaves and always about anti-racism'.

'The things the British did in India and elsewhere are simply not taught in the syllabus and this is a problem,' Dalrymple said. 'When the British go out into the
20 world, they don't know what Indians know about the Raj or what the Irish know about the potato famine, they don't know what the Australians know about the mass extinction of the Indigenous Tasmanians, so we need to teach this in our schools and the opportunity of setting up a museum of colonialism with some of these war criminals and other statues seems to me an opportunity we must take.'

25 The historian Edward Chancellor, also speaking at JLF, disagreed. 'The current statue-bashing is part of the woke movement with its cancel culture, denunciations, forced confessions, censorship, intolerance and profound anti-intellectualism,' he said.

'Give an inch to these people and no statue will be left standing,' he continued. 'It
30 is an assault on the values of the Enlightenment and espouses a cultural nihilism. Behind this is a woke approach to history that is ill-informed, one-sided and anachronistic. It can't understand or accept that different periods have different values and that the historian should strive to be impartial.'

Annotations
08 **topple sth.** make sth. fall
10 **woke** aware of sensitive political issues such as racism or sexism
16 **Henry VIII** English monarch who ruled between 1509 and 1547
16 **Wilberforce** William Wilberforce (1759–1833), leader of the movement to abolish slave trade
20 **Raj** British colonial rule of the Indian subcontinent
30 **Enlightenment** philosophical movement in the 18th century emphasizing the importance of logic and science
30 **espouse sth.** support sth.
30 **nihilism** belief that all values have lost their meaning
31 **anachronistic** out of date

The journalist Swapan Dasgupta, who was also speaking in the debate, was simi-
35 larly against removing statues. 'History was never going to be written on the basis
of how one statue in Bristol looked,' he said. 'This is not an attempt to rewrite
history or make history a little more even-handed. What it really amounts to is
airbrushing history, throwing out a lot of unconformable things, and believing in
sanitising the past to make it palpable to contemporary morality.'

40 Asked if statues in Britain should be removed to a museum of colonialism, 53% of
the debate's audience said they should be, while 47% said they should not.

From: 'UK needs a museum of colonialism, says historian William Dalrymple'
theguardian.com, 16 September 2020

Annotations
39 **palpable** that can be
understood easily

Comprehension

1 What do Dalrymple, Chancellor and Dasgupta think about pulling down statues
from colonial times? Summarize their opinions.

Analysis

2 The article uses several quotations. Explain their functions.

3 Assess which of the opinions you summarized in task **1** comes closest to your
own views.

Language awareness

4 The adjective *woke* is a fairly recent addition to the English lexicon. It has become
widely used, but is also controversial.

a Use a monolingual online dictionary to trace original use and meaning of
woke. Then compare this information to how *woke* is used in the article above
(ll. 10, 26, 31). What differences can you detect?

b Do an internet research to find out how the differences you observed in **a**
came about and why many consider *woke* a problematic term today.

▶ SF 8: Working with
dictionaries, Student's
book p. 273

▶ SF 13: Doing research,
Student's book p. 278

Statue of Edward Colston,
Bristol, England, shortly
before it was toppled

▶ More info

William Wilberforce

▶ SF 13: Doing research,
  Student's book p. 278

▶ Check

▶ Support p. 28

Beyond the text

5 The text alludes to several events in the history of the British Empire.

a Collect the events mentioned in the text and put them in a chronological order.

b Start a timeline of major events in the history of the British Empire based on your results from task **a** and on the information in the info box below.

> **Info**
>
> The **British Empire** was once the largest colonial empire in the world covering nearly one fourth of Earth's land area. Driven by its desire for raw materials and new markets, England started to establish trading outposts abroad as early as the 16th century. Over the next 300 years, more and
> 5 more territories would come under British domination as part of its bid to achieve economic and military superiority. The British Empire reached its peak by around 1920, when it ruled over approximately 20% of the world's population.
> In the aftermath of World War II (1939–1945), many colonies started to
> 10 seek autonomy and political independence. This led to a steady decline of the British Empire. Hong Kong was the last major colony to leave British rule when it was handed back to China in 1997, but Britain still controls some smaller territories around the world even though they aren't officially called colonies.

c Work in groups of three. Each of you is assigned one topic on the British Empire:
  1 William Wilberforce (1759–1833) and the Slavery Abolition Act
  2 Black War (also known as Tasmanian War) (1824–1832)
  3 Irish Potato Famine (1845–1849)

Research your topic and prepare a three-minute talk. Focus on:
  • essential information about the British Empire to be added to your timeline
  • why your topic may or may not have been left out of the history curriculum for British school children.

d `Speaking` Give your talks, then complete your timelines.

5 a Brainstorm reasons why the British Empire came to an end after 1945. Explain your ideas in class.

b `Viewing` Watch a short video clip by the Imperial War Museum in London and check which of your ideas also feature in the clip. Add any new ideas to your notes.

c In small groups, discuss what humankind could learn from Britain's colonial past to create a better future. Write a group statement and present it in class.

Germany's colonial legacy

Before watching a report about the legacy of German colonialism in Namibia, do these tasks.

- ***Quick write:** Note down what you know about the history of German colonialism. Then share your knowledge in class.
- Read the Info box about German colonialism, then do the task.

Info

In the second half of the 19th century, Britain was not the only European power to seek **colonies overseas**. Numerous European countries, including the German Empire, were striving for the acquisition of colonial territories to create new markets for their products, gain access to valuable raw materials and pursue what
5 they thought to be 'civilizing missions' among people they considered backward. When thirteen European powers, together with the United States of America and the Ottoman Empire, met at a conference in Berlin between November 1884 and February 1885, the foundations were laid for the division between them of the African continent. The German Empire, which felt it had been lagging behind other
10 European powers, was allowed to occupy territories in West Africa (today's Togo and parts of Ghana and Cameroon), East Africa (today's Tanzania) and southern Africa (today's Namibia). Later on, in 1898, Germany also leased land in northeast China (around the city of Qingdao) and took possession of many islands in the Pacific. German colonial rulers did not refrain from exploiting and oppressing local
15 people to reach their goals. Among the most gruesome wars fought by the German Empire were the Herero and Nama Wars in present-day Namibia between 1904 and 1908, which ended in the killing of tens of thousands of Hereros and Namas – the first genocide of the 20th century.

1 Explain why the German Empire was eager to have colonies.

Comprehension

1 **a** Listening Work with a partner. While watching, partner A takes notes on the concerns of the Herero community, partner B on the German reactions to them. Compare and discuss your notes.

   b Watch the report again. Explain why Mr. Peringanda feels offended by the inscription on the war monument.

Beyond the text

2 Intercultural communication The report ends by saying that the wounds of German colonialism in Namibia have still not healed. In class, brainstorm ideas on what Germany and Namibia could do to help these wounds to heal.

► Support p. 28

The Commonwealth – family or foe?

• Read the information about the Commonwealth.

► More info

Info

The **Commonwealth** is a voluntary association of 54 countries which work together closely to promote values such as democracy, human rights, education, equality, the rule of law, and peace. It was founded in 1949 by the United Kingdom and seven other independent nations which had formerly been
5 governed by Britain (Australia, Canada, India, New Zealand, Pakistan, South Africa, Sri Lanka). It was subsequently joined by many other countries, most of which had once been part of the British Empire. At present, there are 2.4 billion citizens living in the Commonwealth.

The Commonwealth Secretariat (founded in 1965) represents the interests of
10 member countries and provides support and assistance. It is managed by the Commonwealth Secretary-General, who ensures that the rules of the Commonwealth are followed. Every two years, the leaders of the member countries gather to discuss current global affairs and set their new priorities. The British sovereign has been granted the symbolic role of the head of the Commonwealth.
15 To promote unity, the Commonwealth works hard to bring its member countries together in many different ways, for example, through distance-learning programmes or sports events. Every four years, athletes from across the Commonwealth meet at the Commonwealth Games, the world's first fully inclusive sports event, to compete against each other and celebrate togetherness.

1 Describe the flag of the Commonwealth and try to explain what it symbolizes.

On Commonwealth Day the members of the Commonwealth commemorate their shared history and close ties. It usually takes place on the second Monday in March.

Comprehension

1 a Viewing Watch Prince Charles' message on Commonwealth Day 2021. Note down the topics he addresses in his *speech.
b Viewing Watch the clip again and make notes on each topic.
c Compare your notes with a partner. Together, write a statement in which you sum up the new goals of the Commonwealth envisioned by Prince Charles.

Annotations
'3"43 Terra Carta program started by Prince Charles to promote sustainable development

Analysis

2 The clip makes use of various film techniques. Analyse the functions of the long shots and medium shots used in the clip, of having Prince Charles speak directly to the camera, and of inserting film footage into the video.

► SF 39: Analysing films and videos, Student's book p. 315

Beyond the text

► Check
► SF 26: Argumentative writing, Student's book p. 298

3 Writing The British writer and broadcaster Afua Hirsch has been highly critical of the Commonwealth, calling it *Empire 2.0*. Research Ms. Hirsch's arguments, then write a *comment on them.

Welcome to Nigeria!

- **Partner B**: Look at the pictures on p. 28 and work on the tasks there.
- **Partner A:** Look at the pictures on the right.
- What aspects of Nigerian life are depicted? Which picture comes closer to your notion of Nigeria?
- Share your impressions with your partner and compare them. Together, study the facts in the box and relate them to your photos.
- In class, discuss which facets of Nigeria the photos and the facts do not reveal. *Cluster your unanswered questions on the board.

NIGERIA 🟩 🟩		
POPULATION:		201,000,000
URBAN POPULATION:	51.2%	
POPULATION BELOW POVERTY LINE:	70%	
LIFE EXPECTANCY:	👤 56 years	👤 54 years
LITERACY RATES:		
	FEMALE 52.7% 👤	
	MALE 71.3% 👤	
UNEMPLOYMENT RATE:	8.1%	
RELIGIONS:		
53.5% Muslim	44.9% Christian	

Data taken from: Henning Aubel et al. Der neue Kosmos Welt-Almanach & Atlas. 2020

The clip you are about to watch may offer some surprising facts about Nigeria.

Comprehension

1 a `Listening` Watch the short clip twice and make notes on the following points: geography • people • religion • culture • economy.
  b Check whether the clip has been helpful in answering some of your questions about Nigeria.

Analysis

2 a Nigeria is often referred to as the 'giant of Africa'. Discuss whether the video supports or contradicts this *image.
  b `Viewing` Analyse what means the film uses to present this image of Nigeria.
  c `Intercultural communication` The video's presenter Leroy Kenton is Canadian. Discuss what consequences this may have for the presentation of Nigeria.

▶ Getting started

▶ SF 39: Analysing films and videos, Student's book p. 315

Beyond the text

3 **Art in Context** Visit Nigerian artist Ade Adekola's website and study his series *Icons as transplants* in which he explores the tension between local Nigerian identity and globalization. What new views of Nigeria can you detect? Discuss your ideas in small groups. Then choose your favourite artwork and present it in class.

4 Make your own collage about Nigeria entitled 'Nigeria – multiple perspectives.' You may use facts, images or quotes. Present your collages in a gallery walk.

▶ More info

My vision of Nigeria   Aisha Yesufu

- In 2020 Nigeria celebrated the 60th anniversary of its independence from British colonial rule. The picture shows the logo which was designed especially for that occasion. What could each element in the logo symbolize?

Info

Aisha Yesufu (born 1973) is a prominent Nigerian political activist who has been fighting for justice and equity for many years. In 2014 she was one of the founders of the #BringbackOurGirls movement, which demanded the immediate release of more than 200 schoolgirls who had been kidnapped in northern Nigeria
5 by the Islamist terrorist group Boko Haram. Aisha Yesufu has also spoken out against police brutality in Nigeria. As a businesswoman and founder of the non-profit organization *Citizens Hub,* she promotes financial literacy to empower citizens to become financially independent.

The following text is Aisha Yesufu's contribution to a collection of essays entitled Remaking Nigeria, *published in the year of Nigeria's 60th anniversary.*

Annotations
2 **equity** fairness

Aisha Yesufu

Annotations
05 **perish** die
06 **pale** *(v) (here)* seem less important compared to sth. else
07 **with impunity** without being punished
12 **abduct sb.** take sb. away by force
13 **rig sth.** manipulate sth.
13 **mar sth.** ruin sth.
14 **loot sth.** rob sth.
18 **docile** easy to control
20 **maim sb.** wound sb. causing permanent damage

I see myself someday sitting in a beautifully kept park in a bustling city in Nigeria with my grandchildren, telling them about the Nigeria that was. The Nigeria before they were born; the Nigeria that broke many and made many more lose hope; the Nigeria where young people mostly had one obsession: to leave the country even
5 though many perished trying to cross deserts and seas and some were sold into slavery. Those risks paled in comparison with little or no opportunities while at the mercy of trigger-happy security agents who killed young people with impunity.

I will tell them of the Nigeria where you had to know someone to become somebody and merit was sacrificed for connection; the Nigeria where access to good quality
10 education was dependent on the economic status of one's family. I will tell them of the killings and the lack of value placed on the life of a Nigerian and about girls who were abducted from their school just because they wanted to be educated. [...]

I will tell them of elections rigged and marred by violence that brought in rulers whose main interest was serving themselves and looting public funds. I will tell
15 them of the time the Nigerian President spent months in another country for medical treatment and made Nigeria a laughing stock before the world; a country where the wealth of the nation was looted brazenly at the expense of national development. I will tell them of docile citizens who were too afraid to speak up and fight for a better nation for themselves. They prayed for things God had given them
20 capacity to do for themselves yet killed and maimed in the name of God. They fought for God and left their fight to God. I see myself telling them of the Nigeria where there was so much generational hatred amongst the citizens and people fought for tribal dominance and showed hatred to those not from their place; a nation yearning for identity; a nation which started with potentials for greatness
25 but failed to actualize those potentials.

My grandchildren will look at me and say, 'Stop kidding Grandma. That cannot be true!' [...]

I will look at my grandchildren and smile, knowing full well why they think that I am kidding them. How would they understand a period when many were ashamed
30 to carry the Nigerian passport compared to when many would be doing everything they could to get the Nigerian passport and the opportunities that would come with being a Nigerian? By then, the improved quality of education and the literacy level of citizens would have led to an empowered and enlightened electorate who are able to make informed political decisions and choose candidates based on their
35 competence, character and capacity and not based on their ethnicity, religion or gender. Our best and brightest would then be in leadership positions and not the worst of us as it used to be. Rigging of elections and political thuggery that once marred our elections would be distant memories; little wonder my grandchildren would be enjoying the dividends of democracy: good governance, accountability,
40 and transparency. [...]

Equality and respect are two main factors that would have helped in building the Nigeria of my grandchildren. Gone would be the days when Nigerians fought over tribal and religious superiority. What will matter in the Nigeria of my grandchildren will be our identity as Nigerians and not our ethnic identities as Efik, Igbo,
45 Yoruba, Hausa, Fulani, Ijaw, Ogoni, Tiv, Ebira, etc. Everyone will have the opportunity to key into the Nigerian dream without discrimination. Citizens will be accorded respect and dignity. The life of every Nigerian will be worthy of the attention of the state and will be protected at all costs. The Nigeria of my grandchildren will have citizens that will give their all to their country and will be ready to die for it. A
50 country that dignifies you will have your loyalty.

Looking around in the park with my grandchildren, it will be hard to believe that Nigeria was once the poverty capital of the world, a country where unemployment was once so high and infrastructural development so minimal. How are my grandchildren to comprehend how citizens endured not having regular electricity or that
55 there were children like them that roamed the streets, abandoned by their parents and that many who should have called for the system that kept them on the street to be abolished, supported it? Or that it was like a crime to be poor in Nigeria of the past and the only time that the poor mattered was during election where their thumbprints could be exploited for pittance. We would truly have come a long way
60 as a nation; our perseverance led us this far. We would once again be the happiest people on earth. [...]

Many will say these are pipe dreams. As I look at the reality of Nigeria as we celebrate our 60th year of independence, a part of me wants to agree with them and just give up the fight for a new and better Nigeria. But then, there is a stronger part
65 of me that sees the Nigeria of my grandchildren being a reality. Giving up on Nigeria is so easy; it means we do not have to do anything other than complain and keep looking for an opportunity to leave the country and go to countries that were once in the situation we are in today but had citizens who refused to give up and believed in having a functional and prosperous nation and worked hard to achieve it.

70 Looking at the great possibility of what Nigeria can be and believing in that possibility is a lot harder. It means we must do our bit to get the Nigeria that we deserve.

Annotations
33 **electorate** all people who are allowed to vote
37 **thuggery** brutal crime
47 **dignity** the fact of being given respect
59 **pittance** very small amount of money
60 **perseverance** [ˌpɜːsəˈvɪərəns] continued effort despite difficulties
62 **pipe dream** fantastic or unrealistic plan

We must never set goals based on our present reality but based on what we want. A prosperous and great Nigeria is something that many of us want even when there are many who think it is not achievable. It is! The first and most important
75 step is to believe. Let us collectively do what we can to achieve this new Nigeria we yearn for. We can achieve that by working together rather than working against one another. In the words of Nelson Mandela, the first black president of South Africa, 'It always seems impossible, until it's done.'

I know that the Nigeria of today is not our destiny. There is a Nigeria for the unborn
80 generation that we should fight for just as others fought to make Nigeria independent sixty years ago. We cannot afford to give up on that Nigeria.

I know by the grace of God Almighty,

#NigeriaMustWorkInOurLifetime.

From: The Nigeria that I see, *in: Remaking Nigeria. Sixty Years, Sixty Voices, 2020.*

▶ SF 17: Reading and understanding non-fictional texts, Student's book p. 285

▶ Check 👆

A protester during a demonstration against police brutality in Lagos, Nigeria

▶ Support p. 29

Comprehension

1 a Summarize the problems of contemporary Nigeria and the country's potential as Aisha Yesufu sees them.

b Ms. Yesufu alludes to several events in modern Nigerian history. Match the events below to passages in her *essay and explain why she uses these historical allusions.
- *Nigerian Civil War (1967–1970):* a war fought between the central government and the Republic of Biafra, which was set up by nationalists of the Igbo ethnic group in an attempt to declare independence from Nigeria
- *Chibok schoolgirls kidnapping (2014):* abduction of more than 270 mostly Christian girls aged between 16 and 18 by the Islamist terrorist group Boko Haram
- *Nigerian refugee crisis (since 2014):* displacement of 2.4 million people since Boko Haram's attacks started
- *President Buhari's stay abroad (2017):* extended medical treatment of the Nigerian president in the UK, lasting for more than 100 days

Analysis

2 Ms. Yesufu emphasizes the importance of national identity for Nigeria's future while downplaying the importance of ethnic identity. Analyse how she does so and why.

> **Language help**
> personal pronoun • include/exclude sb. from … • contrast sth. to • refer to sb. as … • use proper names

3 a Ms. Yesufu uses the phrase 'I will tell them …' repeatedly in her essay. Explain the intended effect. Then give more examples of *repetition and parallel structures in the essay.

b Write a short paragraph in which you imagine what you will tell your grandchildren about your home country in sixty years' time. Use repetition and parallel structures.

4 a Note down the main features of Aisha Yesufu's Nigerian dream.

b Challenge Speaking Compare Aisha Yesufu's Nigerian Dream with the American Dream. Give a 2-minute talk about them.

Welcome to Singapore!

- Singapore has several nicknames. Look at the two pictures and guess what the following nicknames could mean: *The Little Red Dot, The Garden City, The Lion City, The Asian Tiger, The Fine City*. Do an internet research of how Singapore got its nicknames and check whether your initial ideas were correct.

- Read the Info box about Singapore.

Info

The city state of **Singapore**, home to nearly 6 million citizens, is one of the most prosperous countries in the world. It consists of Singapore Island (Malay 'Pulau Ujong', meaning 'land's end') and more than 60 smaller islands in the Malayan archipelago. Legend has it that Singapore received its name from a Sumatran
5 prince who reigned over the region in the 14th century. While on a hunt the prince encountered a big animal, which his advisors believed to be a lion. This eventually led to renaming the region 'Singapura', meaning 'lion'. Ironically, the animal that the prince might have spotted was probably a Malayan tiger, as lions never lived in this part of the world.
10 Modern Singapore dates back to the early 19th century. In 1819, Sir Thomas Stamford Raffles, a British statesman, negotiated a treaty with local rulers that

allowed the British to open a new trading port on the island, which was located at a strategically important position along the sea route between British India and China. The port developed quickly, drawing more and more immigrants from
15   China, India and the Malayan archipelago to its shores. Half a decade later, in 1867, Singapore became a crown colony.

In World War I (1914–18) Singaporean life was not affected significantly, whereas in World War II (1939–45) it was impacted greatly. In the Battle of Singapore (February 1942), British forces were defeated by the Japanese Empire, which
20   would occupy the territory for the following three years and rename it 'Syonan-to' ('light of the south' in Japanese). After the war, Singapore was returned to the British, who granted the people of Singapore more self-government when demands for self-rule became stronger. It was not before 1965, however, that Singapore finally became an independent republic.

25   The new Singaporean government, headed by Prime Minister Lee Kuan Yew, was highly successful at modernizing the country, which led to an unprecedented economic boom greatly admired by other postcolonial nations whose transition to independence proceeded less smoothly. By the 1990s, Singapore had become one of the world's richest nations. Today Singapore is praised for its political
30   stability, its security, its education system, its economic competitiveness coupled with sustainable development – and its cleanliness! Critics, on the other hand, argue that Singapore is not truly democratic, pointing to the fact that Singapore has, since independence, been dominated by only one party, the People's Action Party (PAP), and accusing the government of neocolonial authoritarianism and
35   repression of oppositional voices.

Singaporeans are proud of their multiethnic, multicultural and multireligious heritage, which is reflected in the city's architecture, art, food, and festivals. Ethnic Chinese comprise three-fourths of Singapore's total population today, with Malays and Indians coming second and third. Far from homogenous, each
40   community speaks a wealth of different languages and dialects. The official languages of Singapore are Mandarin Chinese, Malay, Tamil, and English. As the language of the former colonizers, English is the main medium for administration and business and is also the preferred language of instruction in Singapore's schools and universities.

1   Mention two aspects that surprised you, two that you already knew about Singapore and two that were new to you. Talk about your lists with a partner.

• Discuss whether Singapore's development could serve as a model for the future of other independent nations that were once part of the British Empire.

The poem 'Bumboat cruise on the Singapore River' by Miriam Wei Wei Lo on the next page takes readers on a cruise down Singapore River, a popular tourist attraction.

Info

Miriam Wei Wei Lo (born 1973) is an Australian poet who considers herself 'complicated'. Born in Canada to a Chinese-Malaysian father and an Anglo-Australian mother, she grew up in Singapore and then moved to Australia to study. Today she lives in Western Australia. She has published several collections of poetry and a children's book which reflect many aspects of her own cultural heritage and cross-cultural experiences.

Bumboat cruise on the Singapore River   Miriam Wei Wei Lo

Rhetoric is what keeps this island afloat.
Singaporean voice with a strong American accent,
barely audible above the drone of the bumboat engine:
'Singaporeans are crazy about their food.
5 They are especially fond of all-you-can-eat buffets.
Why not do as the locals do and try out one of the buffets
at these hotels along the waterfront.' The Swissotel looms.
The Grand Copthorne. The Miramar. All glass
and upward-sweeping architecture. Why not do
10 as the locals do. Here in this city where conspicuous consumption
is an artform. Where white tourists wearing slippers and singlets
are tolerated in black-tie establishments. Dollars. Sense.

How did I ever live in this place? Sixteen years of my life
afloat in this sea of contradictions, of which I was, equally, one:
15 half-white, half-Chinese; the taxi-driver cannot decide
if I am a tourist or a local, so he pitches at my husband:
'Everything in Singapore is changing all the time.'
Strong gestures. Manic conviction. 'This is good.
We are never bored. Sometimes my customers
20 ask me to take them to a destination, but it is no longer there.'
We tighten our grip on two squirming children and pray
that the bumboat tour will exist. Nothing short of a miracle
this small wooden boat which is taking us now past Boat Quay,
in its current incarnation, past the Fullerton Hotel

25 To the mouth of the Singapore river, where the Merlion
still astonishes: grotesque and beautiful as a gargoyle.
The children begin to chafe at confinement. My daughter wails
above the drone of the engine. There's talk of closing the mouth
of the river. New water supply. There's talk of a casino.
30 Heated debate in the Cabinet. Old Lee and Young Lee
locked in some Oedipal battle. The swell is bigger out here
in the harbour, slapping up spray against the sides of the boat,
as if it were waves that kept it afloat, this boat,
this island, caught between sinking and swimming,
35 as I am caught now. As if rhetoric mattered.
As if this place gives me a name for myself.

From: Westerly, 2005

Annotations
10 **conspicuous** striking, easy to notice
11 **singlet** sleeveless undershirt
18 **manic** very excited
21 **squirm** move around uncomfortably or nervously
24 **incarnation** *(here)* state, condition
25 **Merlion** mythical creature that is half mermaid, half lion spouting water into the Singapore River; Singapore's mascot and one of its most famous landmarks
26 **gargoyle** ugly figure made of stone, usually spouting rainwater from a roof
27 **chafe at sth.** be annoyed and impatient about sth. because it limits you
30 **Old Lee** Lee Kuan Yew, Singapore's first Prime Minister up until 1995
30 **Young Lee** Lee Hsien Long, became Prime Minister in 2004
31 **Oedipal** [ˈiːdɪpl/] *(here)* psychologically complex

Comprehension

1 Read the poem to find out …
- who is taking the bumboat cruise
- what happens before the tour starts
- which sights can be seen from the boat
- what they learn about Singapore

- what the boat ride makes the *speaker think of
- how the boat ride makes the speaker feel.

► SF 19: Reading and understanding poetry, Student's book p. 287

► Check

Quote lines from the poem.

Analysis

2 a The poem uses the word 'rhetoric' twice to describe contemporary Singapore and the Singaporean lifestyle (ll. 1, 35). Explain this lexical choice in the context of the poem.

b Analyse the *speaker's ambivalent relationship to Singapore. Take into account the following aspects: What ties the speaker to the country? What aspects does the speaker find perplexing? And how does this affect the speaker's sense of self?

Language awareness

▶ More language 👆

▶ SF 36: Creative writing, Student's book p. 311

3 a Explain the use of the present progressive 'is changing all the time' (l. 17).

b Writing Put yourself in the situation of the speaker on the bumboat and write a short *interior monologue. Use the present progressive with *all the time* or *always*.

Beyond the text

▶ SF 36: Creative writing, Student's book p. 311

▶ SF 41: Giving a presentation, Student's book p. 321

4 You choose Work on either of the tasks below.

a Writing Work with a partner. Imagine after a long day of sightseeing in Singapore the speaker calls a very good friend in Australia and talks about their day. Do some research, then write their *dialogue and act it out.

b Intercultural communication Singapore's cuisine is as diverse as its cultures. In small groups, prepare short presentations on popular, multicultural Singaporean dishes.

Text 7

Smart Nation Singapur – die digitale Stadt   Christoph Hein

• What is your vision of a 'smart nation' or 'smart city'? Brainstorm ideas.

Der strenge Stadtstaat vernetzt sich wie kein anderes Land der Erde. Schon heute geht fast alles mit dem Handy. Dazu braucht es visionäre Politiker – und folgsame Bürger.

Morgens gegen elf Uhr lässt Benedikt Tschörner Manila überfluten. „Andere
5 reden vom Anstieg des Meeresspiegels, wir zeigen ihn", sagt er. Dann schiebt Tschörner den Regler am linken Rand des riesigen Bildschirms noch höher, das digitale Stadtbild färbt sich blau und blauer. „Der Klimawandel wird dazu führen, dass große Stadtgebiete Manilas in 80 Jahren überflutet sein werden, wird nicht sehr schnell etwas getan", sagt der Entwickler des Fraunhofer Instituts in Singapur.
10 Die philippinische Hauptstadt gilt den Informatikern im Stadtstaat nur als Testobjekt ihrer Methoden. Eigentlich arbeiten sie am drohenden Überschwemmungs-Szenario Singapurs. Sehen dürfen das aber bislang nur Auserwählte. „Die Bevölkerung wird die Auswirkungen später in Simulationsräumen erleben können", sagt Tschörner. „Zunächst liefern wir den Entscheidern Grundlagen."

15 Virtuelle Stadtmodelle für die Modellstadt sind nur ein Hilfsmittel, das die Singapurer nutzen auf ihrem Weg, aus ihrer Smart City eine Smart Nation zu

machen. In der Tropenstadt ohne eigene Bodenschätze wird groß gedacht. Auch in Punggol. Fast 200 Jahre ist es her, da zogen die Malaien hier Fruchtbäume hoch. „Punggol", der Stadtteil im Nordosten Singapurs, steht für die Stecken, welche die
20 Bäume damals beim Wachstum stützten. Heute lassen hier chinesische Baukonzerne immer mehr Hochhäuser für 160.000 Menschen heranwachsen. Zu ihren Füßen entsteht der Punggol Digital District: 50 Hektar, 28.000 Arbeitsplätze, 12.000 Studenten – ein Leitbild für die Smart Nation Singapur. [...]

Schon jetzt hat Singapur auf dem Weg zur Smart Nation viel erreicht, mehr als fast
25 alle anderen Städte dieser Welt. Steuererklärung? Dauert hier nur zwanzig Minuten am Bildschirm, weil man nur Veränderungen gegenüber dem Vorjahr angeben muss. [...]

Für fast alles ist digital gesorgt. Eintrittskarte in die schöne neue Digitalwelt am Äquator ist der Sing-
30 Pass. Wie das „Sesam öffne dich" bei Ali Baba und den 40 Räubern öffnet er die Tür zu den Ämtern des Staates – Klicks und Passwörter sind Vergangenheit. [...] Der SingPass aber bildet nur die Oberfläche, welche die Bürger direkt nutzen. Dahinter wächst in
35 Hochgeschwindigkeit eine virtuelle Welt heran: Für Punggol, aber auch den kommenden Stadtteil Jurong Innovation District mit seinen 600 Hektar, nutzen die Entwickler immer häufiger „Digital Twins", virtuelle Zwillinge der Wirklichkeit. „Beim
40 Bau von Fabriken unter dem Konzept Industrie 4.0 ist das ja üblich. Der Bau ganzer Stadtteile zunächst am Bildschirm ist dann aber noch mal viel kompli-

zierter", sagt Wolfgang Müller-Wittig. Der Professor und Standortleiter des Ablegers der Deutschen Fraunhofer Gesellschaft im fünften Stock der Nanyang
45 Technological University unterstützt Singapur seit 20 Jahren auf dessen Weg in die digitale Zukunft. [...]

„Die Smart Nation hat so viele Aspekte", sagt Müller-Wittig. Wie auch Tan im JTC-Turm meint er: „Der Weg muss nun dahin führen, die Systeme immer weiter zusammenzubinden, und das mit so wenigen Daten wie nur möglich." Das
50 Zusammenführen aber gilt nicht nur für Daten: „Singapur scannt die Welt und holt sich dann die besten Talente." [...]

Ist das Ziel zu erkennen, wissen Forscher und Manager indes, dass der Weg dorthin weit ist. Kein Bereich Singapurs bleibt unberührt. Das aber sorgt auch für Risiken. Sie scheinen nicht allen im Stadtstaat jederzeit bewusst, und die Deu-
55 tungshoheit gibt, wie immer, die seit Staatsgründung 1965 amtierende Regierungspartei vor. Zehntausende zusätzliche Kameras zur Überwachung der kleinsten Regung der Bürger? Kein Problem, sichern sie ja unser aller Sicherheit. Die rasante Zunahme digitaler Diebstähle, bei denen Täter auch über Tage unbemerkt Tausende von Dollar von Privatkonten bei Asiens „bester digitaler Bank", der DBS
60 Group, abräumen? Das ist schlecht, die Aufklärung dauert neun Monate, die Erstattung durch die Bank ist ungewiss – Singapur aber beginnt eine Kampagne, die vor Datendiebstahl warnt. [...]

Wer glaubt, der Stadt ginge es bei all dem nur um bessere Dienstleistungen für ihre Bürger, kennt Singapur nicht. Die Digitalisierung wirft mindestens zwei 65 Nebeneffekte ab: Der Stadtstaat gilt als eine der am besten überwachten Gesellschaften der Welt. Was aber in China anstößig wirkt, wird hier immer noch als hilfreich und schützend verstanden. Weniger umstritten ist der Abstrahleffekt auf das Ausland: Noch sind die übrigen neun südostasiatischen Länder in weiten Teilen unterentwickelt – Singapur ist den Nachbarländern meilenweit voraus. 70 Wird die Digitalisierung gepaart mit Industrie 4.0, mit Robotik, mit Energie-, Medizin- oder Nahrungstechnik, wird immer öfter Künstliche Intelligenz zum Einsatz kommen, wachsen die Exportchancen. [...]

Läuft alles gut, dürfen sich Bosch in Stuttgart und der TÜV Süd im fernen München ein kleines Stück von der Zukunft Singapurs als Smart Nation abschnei- 75 den. Immer dann, wenn in einem Gebäude auf der Insel ein Aufzug herauf- oder herunterfährt, will ein Team der beiden die Daten erheben, um dank der Fernwartung drohende Ausfälle frühzeitig zu erkennen – bevor es zu einem Unfall kommen kann. [...]

„Hier in Singapur sind sie Deutschland um Meilen voraus. Ich wünschte mir, dass 80 man sich dort ein Stück von Singapur abschnitte", sagt Tschörner, während er seinen Datenhelm im Fraunhofer Institut zur Seite legt. Er hält inne. „Die Regierung hier hat sich alle Mittel gesichert, mit denen sie theoretisch den übelsten Horrorstaat der Welt bauen könnte. Dieser Grad der Digitalisierung geht aus meiner Sicht überhaupt nur, weil die Regierung hier in Singapur so ordentlich 85 arbeitet."

From: Frankfurter Allgemeine Zeitung, *31 May 2021*

▶ Getting started
▶ SF 47: Mediating written and oral texts, Student's book p. 332

1 Mediating Imagine you are an intern at Germany's Fraunhofer Institute in Singapore. Summarize for your Singaporean colleagues what the article says about how Singapore tries to improve the quality of life for its citizens and what Germany could learn from it.

▶ More info

Info

Johnny Cash (1932–2003) was one of the most popular U.S. singer-songwriters in the history of American music. His music covers a wide range of *genres, including country, rock, and blues, which he mixed innovatively to create a unique hybrid sound.

Forty shades of green   Johnny Cash

- Finish this sentence in as many ways as possible: *When I think of Ireland I think of …*
- Compare your ideas with at least three other classmates.
- In class, cluster your ideas about Ireland.

In 1959 Johnny Cash wrote the song 'Forty shades of green' while on a trip to Ireland. The song has become a classic both in the U.S. and in Ireland.

I close my eyes and picture the
   emerald of the sea
From the fishing boats at Dingle to
   the shores of Dunardee
5 I miss the river Shannon and the
   folks at Skibbereen
The moorlands and the meadows
   with their forty shades of green

But most of all I miss a girl in
10 Tipperary town
And most of all I miss her lips as soft
   as eiderdown
Again I want to see and do the things
   we've done and seen
15 Where the breeze is sweet as
   Shalimar and there's forty shades of
   green

I wish that I could spend an hour at
   Dublin's churning surf
20 I'd love to watch the farmers drain
   the bogs and spade the turf
To see again the thatching of the
   straw the women glean
I'd walk from Cork to Larne to see the
25 forty shades of green

But most of all I miss a girl in
   Tipperary town
And most of all I miss her lips as soft
   as eiderdown
30 Again, I want to see and do the things
   we've done and seen
Where the breeze is sweet as
   Shalimar and there's forty shades of
   green

Annotations
12 **eiderdown** [ˈaɪdədaʊn] warm bedcover filled with feathers
16 **Shalimar** a French perfume
19 **churning surf** *(here)* waves rolling in
21 **bog** area of wet, muddy ground that is formed of dead plants
23 **glean sth.** collect sth.

Comprehension

1 a On a map of Ireland, mark the locations that are mentioned in the song.
  b Describe the image of Ireland created in the song.

Analysis

2 Analyse the *speaker's emotions and feelings.

Language awareness

3 a Ireland is referred to as 'the emerald of the sea' (l. 2). Explain this *metaphor and research the story of how Ireland came to be known as 'the Emerald Isle'.
  b Find a photo depicting an interesting aspect of Irish life and write a suitable caption describing Ireland metaphorically. Present your photos and captions in class.

▶ SF 13: Doing research, Student's book p. 278

Beyond the text

4 You choose Work on either task **a** or **b**.

  a Give reasons why 'Forty shades of green' may have been so popular for many decades. Does the song appeal to you, too?

  b There are many popular songs about Ireland. Find one that you particularly like. Why does it appeal to you?

▶ Getting started (task b)

  c Speaking Read the Info box on page 24. Then choose one of the protest songs mentioned in the text and investigate the story behind the song. What other perspectives on Ireland do these songs offer? Report back to class.

▶ SF 13: Doing research, Student's book p. 278

Info

Irish protest songs – an intriguing part of Ireland's musical tradition

Ireland has a very rich musical tradition, and protest songs are an intrinsic part of it. Throughout history, music has helped the Irish express their national identity and give voice to those who would fight against injustice. Many modern Irish songs prove that this tradition lives on today. Protest songs dealing with
5 more recent aspects of Irish history include 'Banana Republic' (1980) by the Boomtown Rats, 'Sunday Bloody Sunday' (1983) by U2, 'Streets of Sorrow/ Birmingham Six' (1988) by The Pogues, 'This Is a Rebel Song' (1997) by Sinead O'Connor and 'Dublin Town' by Damien Dempsey (from 1997).

1 Choose one of the protest songs and find out what it's criticizing.

Text 9

Democratic disruption. Ireland's colonial hangover Bill Rolston

- On the first-ever state visit of a President of the Republic of Ireland to the United Kingdom in April 2014, President Michael D. Higgins (cf. info box on p. 25) described the relationship between the two nations as follows: 'Ireland and Britain live in both the shadow and in the shelter of one another, and so it has been since the dawn of history.' Explain this quote in your own words. Then share what you know about the 'shadows' and 'shelters' connecting the two countries. The pictures can help you.

Now read the text by Bill Rolston, a Northern Irish scholar. Much of his research deals with Ireland's ways of coping with its past.

In 1991 a Northern Ireland based NGO, the Centre for Research and Documentation, organised a conference in Dublin titled 'Is Ireland a Third World Country?' The question [...] was deliberately provocative. In one sense, the answer was clearly 'no'.
5 Ireland is not in the Global South. Dublin is the capital of a sovereign democratic state. There were economic problems, but no one was starving to death openly on the streets. And although a relatively low-intensity war [was] happening, it was happening in Northern Ireland, the part which stayed integrated in the
10 British political system when Ireland was partitioned in the 1920s.

On the other hand, in those years before the economic boom, known as 'the Celtic Tiger', the southern part of the island of Ireland was a very different place from what it is now. In 1841 the population of the whole, unpartitioned island was about
15 eight million. A devastating famine followed where two million or more died or emigrated. A century and a half later, despite a birth rate higher than [in] most other European countries, the population was less than six million. Even today,

Annotations
15 **famine** shortage of food

after the arrival of tens of thousands of European Union citizens and others, the island's population has not yet reached the pre-Famine level. The main reason for
20 low population figures during the 90s was the extent of emigration. London, New York, Melbourne were teeming with young Irish people holding down successful jobs. They were not able to thrive in Ireland where employment opportunities were severely restricted. Economically, Ireland was acknowledged as the basket case of the European Union.

The colonisation of Ireland
25 When the South of Ireland achieved independence from Britain in 1922, it carried the baggage of centuries of colonial rule. The Normans had begun to conquer Ireland in the late 12th century. For the next five hundred years there was an uneasy relationship between Ireland and England which involved both incorporation and
30 resistance. The Elizabethans determined to complete the conquest in the late 17th century, subduing the northern clans through a combination of war and plantation. Throughout much of the 18th and 19th centuries, English laws blocked the development of any indigenous industry which might challenge English economic dominance. Repressive control was 'normal' as resistance against conquest contin-
35 ued; in the second half of the 19th century the rule of law, unencumbered by emergency or martial measures, existed for only five years. Resistance reached its zenith with the Easter Rising in 1916, which was followed by the War of Independence from 1919 to 1921, the Treaty and the Government of Ireland Act 1920 which led to the partition of the island. The 26 southern counties – the Free State – were
40 now a dominion within the British sphere of influence, while the six northern counties – Northern Ireland – had its own parliament but remained fully incorporated within the United Kingdom.

Repressive control and monopoly of power
The newly 'independent' Free State in the south was not really so. The young state
45 would in time flex its muscles: it refused to join the British Commonwealth and declared military neutrality, it supported China, Palestine and Cuba in the United Nations; and in 1949 it declared itself a republic. But it was in many ways still a neo-colonial set-up.

The situation in Northern Ireland remained much more obviously colonial af-
50 ter 1921. In an attempt at counterinsurgency in the early 17th century, thousands of settlers had been brought in. Scottish, English-speaking and Presbyterian they had displaced the Gaelic-speaking, Catholic Irish from their land and the repercussions remain to this day. In 1921, the newly partitioned state got its own government, albeit subordinate to Britain, where the unionists,
55 ultimately descendants from the original settlers, established a monopoly on power and control. Laws and policies kept the Catholics, ultimately the descendants of the original displaced indigenous, down. They experienced discrimination in the exercise of democratic rights, in access to employment and public housing, and a much higher rate of emigration. Eventually a civil
60 rights campaign in the late 1960s morphed into a three-way war between pro-United Ireland nationalists, pro-British unionists, and British armed forces.

Annotations

31 **plantation** colonization

33 **indigenous** *(here)* local

35 **unencumbered** without any burden

50 **counterinsurgency** military actions against revolutionaries

51 **Presbyterian** member of the Presbyterian church, a Protestant Christian church

52 **Gaelic** Celtic language spoken in Ireland, Wales and Scotland

53 **repercussion** effect

54 **albeit** [ɔːlˈbiːɪt] although

54 **unionist** *(here)* supporter of Northern Ireland's union with Great Britain

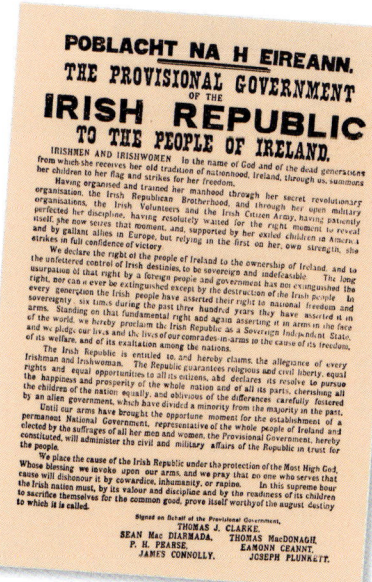

Proclamation of Irish Independence during the Easter Rising 1916

Annotations

70 in perpetuity forever

73 intransigence stubbornness; the quality in people not willing to compromise

Ireland's legacy of colonialism

But it is not simply about the past. The legacy of colonialism continues to work
65 itself out on the island of Ireland and especially in the north. A substantial proportion of the nationalist (Catholic) population regard the partition of the island a century ago as an imperial move that stranded them in a state in which they had no desire to belong. The state was built on inequality. When the unionists were planning where to draw the border, they opted for an area which would, in their words,
70 guarantee them 'a Protestant majority in perpetuity'. The roots of the low-intensity war from 1969 to 1994 are in that experience. The conflict was kick-started by demands for equality in a Civil Rights campaign in the late 1960s which was met with state intransigence and repression.

To this day, demands for equality continue to disrupt the operations of the state.
75 For example, a power-sharing government and executive which resulted from the peace agreement, the Good Friday Agreement, of 1998, collapsed in 2016 over a number of issues, including strong evidence of the corruption of unionist politicians. The other main partner in the executive, the republicans, withdrew over this and other issues. Another example is the determination of the unionists to block
80 an Irish Language Act. Gaelic has declined in many of the areas where it was once dominant, especially in the rural west of Ireland. But it has grown exponentially in urban areas in the north. There are language acts in the Irish Republic, Scotland and Wales protecting indigenous languages. The north is the only outlier, and that because of unionist intransigence. This is one of the reasons the republicans are in
85 no hurry to re-establish the power-sharing institutions.

For all that Ireland is not a developing country, it bears scars similar to those of other post-colonial countries in the Global South. It was colonised, and the legacy of colonialism continues to disrupt democratic processes to the present day. The process of decolonisation remains incomplete, most obviously in Northern Ireland
90 but also in the Republic. As Brexit threatens the economics and politics of these two neighbours, Britain and Ireland, there are many commentators who now argue that Ireland's economic development and political health depend on the ending of partition and the reunification of the country within the European Union. This would be a significant step on the road to decolonisation.

From: https://blogs.lse.ac.uk

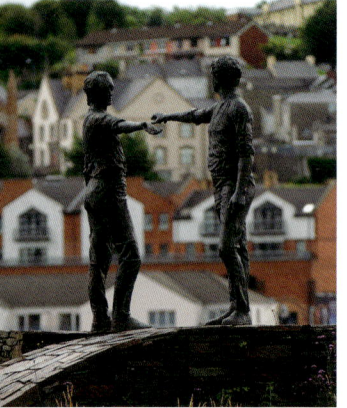

Hands Across the Divide monument, symbolizing the reconciliation between Protestants and Catholics in the Northern Ireland conflict

▶ Getting started 📥

▶ Check 📥

▶ Support p. 29

▶ SF 17: Reading and understanding non-fictional texts, Student's book p. 285

Comprehension

1 a Read the text. Then put the following events from Irish history in chronological order:
Brexit • Good Friday Agreement • Irish Famine • Irish Free State • Partition • troubles in Northern Ireland • Celtic Tiger • Republic of Ireland.

b Read the text again and make notes on the events in **a**.

c 📖 Summarize the colonial legacies that, in the author's view, are still affecting Ireland today.

Analysis

2 Examine the author's intent in writing this article.

3 a Explain how the author's view of Irish history is reflected in his choice of the phrases 'the basket case of the European Union' (l. 23 f.) and 'the island of Ireland' (l. 13).

b Find another sentence in the article reflecting the author's position through his choice of words. Rewrite it using more neutral words.

4 `Writing` Write a comment on another quote by Irish President Michael D. Higgins, published in *The Guardian* in 2021. Bear the guiding question in mind.

▶ SF 26: Argumentative writing, Student's book p. 298

> It is vital to understand the nature of the British imperialist mindset of that time if we are to understand the history of coexisting support for, active resistance to, and, for most, a resigned acceptance of British rule in Ireland. While our nations have been utterly transformed over the past century, I suggest that there are important benefits for all on these islands of engaging with the shadows cast by our shared past.

`Info`

Michael D. Higgins (born 1941), a socialist, poet, academic and human rights advocate, was inaugurated as the 9th President of Ireland in 2011. On several occasions President Higgins has criticized British imperialism and the refusal of British academic institutions and media organizations to address its colonial
5 legacy. He believes that the distressing aspects of Britain's and Ireland's shared history need to be acknowledged to create a better future for both countries.

▶ More info

Chapter task

A time capsule is a box containing items that store essential information for future generations.
Create a time capsule for an English-speaking country using written information.

1 Form groups of four. Each group chooses one country you dealt with in this chapter. Choose five items that could help future generations understand this country's past and present and put them in a box.

2 Present your items in class and comment on them. What story does your time capsule tell?

Text 1

► p. 10

Does Britain need a museum of colonialism?

5 c Support

In your discussion, you may address the following aspects:
- what Britain's past mistakes were
- how it treated conquered peoples and nations
- what it should do to make up for past mistakes
- how similar mistakes could be avoided
- what today's major powers –the United States, China, the European Union– could learn from the British experience
- what international relations should be like today
- what nations could do to build lasting peace.

Text 2

► p. 11

Germany's colonial legacy

2 Support

Use the words in the box to generate ideas.

> **Language help**
>
> issue an apology • give development aid • build a monument • talk to victims' families • acknowledge/recognize sth. • compensate for sth. • pay reparations • educate sb. about sth.

Text 4

► p. 13

Welcome to Nigeria!

Partner B

- **Partner B:** What aspects of Nigerian life are depicted in the picture below and the one on the next page? Which picture comes closer to your notion of Nigeria?

Go back to p. 13.

Text 5

My vision of Nigeria

▶ p. 16

2 Support

In your analysis, consider the following aspects:
- how often Ms. Yesufu refers to 'Nigeria' and 'Nigerians'
- how often she refers to Nigeria's separate ethnic groups
- which other proper names she uses in the text
- who she means by 'we'.

Text 9

Democratic disruption. Ireland's colonial hangover

▶ p. 26

2 Support

In your analysis, consider the following aspects:
- Statements of opinion or emotional appeals are often used by authors to persuade readers of their own opinions.
- Humorous details and personal anecdotes are often used to create interest, to entertain or to lend credibility to what is said.
- Descriptive passages or statistics are used to inform readers.

Which strategies are employed in the given text?

Abbreviations and labels used in *Context*

AE/BE	American English / British English
ca. *(Latin)*	circa = about, approximately
cf.	confer (compare), see
derog	derogatory *(abfällig, geringschätzig)*
e.g. *(Latin)*	exempli gratia = for example
esp.	especially
et al. *(Latin)*	et alii = and other people/things
etc. *(Latin)*	et cetera = and so on
f./ff.	and the following page(s)/line(s)
fml	formal English
i.e. *(Latin)*	id est = that is, in other words
infml	informal English
jdm./jdn.	*jemandem/jemanden*
l./ll.	line/lines
n	noun
pt(s)	point(s)
p./pp.	page/pages
pl	plural
sb./sth.	somebody/something
sin	singular
sl	slang
usu.	usually
v	verb
vs.	*(Latin)* versus *(gegen, im Gegensatz zu)*

🗺	marks tasks that refer you back to the chapter's guiding question
Challenge	marks a more difficult task
▶ Support	refers you to the Support and Partner B pages (p. 28f.) where you can find more help to do the assignment
You choose	lets you decide which of the two given assignments you'd like to do
Intercultural communication	marks a task that focuses on intercultural communication
* metaphor	indicates that a word or expression (here: *metaphor*) is explained in the Glossary in the Student's book *Context*, p. 334ff.
▶ SF 48: Paraphrasing	directs you to the Skills File in the Student's book *Context*, p. 264ff. (here: Skill 48)
🔊	indicates that the sound file can be found in the Cornelsen Lernen App, eBook and UMA
▶	indicates that the video can be found in the Cornelsen Lernen App, eBook and UMA
▶ More info ↙	indicates that additional information can be found in the Cornelsen Lernen App
▶ More language ↙	indicates that tips or further information regarding language can be found in the Cornelsen Lernen App
▶ Check ↙	indicates that solutions to tasks can be found in the Cornelsen Lernen App
▶ Getting started ↙	indicates that tips or ideas to get started on tasks can be found in the Cornelsen Lernen App

Cover

Shutterstock.com/mehdi33300

Photos

pp. 4/5 and details: mauritius images/Art Collection 2/Alamy Stock Photos; **p. 9:** stock.adobe.com/Chris Sharp; **p. 10:** mauritius images/World Book Inc.; **p. 12:** Shutterstock.com/Luketaibai; **p. 13** top: stock.adobe.com/Bassey, bottom left map and flag: stock.adobe.com/Khaiinauy, people icons: Shutterstock.com/Design Collection, bottom right: stock.adobe.com/ Fela Sanu; **p. 14** top: Shutterstock.com/saw graf, bottom: dpa Picture-Alliance/REUTERS/X02952/JOE PENNEY; **p. 16**: mauritius images/alamy stock photo/Majority World CIC; **p. 17** left: stock.adobe.com/Noppasinw, right: stock.adobe.com/ Zerophoto; **p. 18**: ClipDealer GmbH/Andriy Kravchenko; **p. 19**: Shutterstock.com/haireena; **p. 21**: mauritius images/alamy stock photo/Kiyoshi Hijiki; **p. 22**: mauritius images/TopFoto; **p. 24** top: mauritius images/alamy stock photo/Magdalena Gierlik, bottom: Imago Stock & People GmbH/imageBROKER/Matthias Graben; **p. 25**: mauritius images/World Book Inc.; **p. 26**: mauritius images/alamy stock photo/Zoonar GmbH; **p. 27**: mauritius images/alamy stock photo/Graham Service; **p. 28**: stock.adobe.com/Terver, **p. 29**: stock.adobe.com/Артем Малахов

Texts

pp. 8–9 Flood, Alison. "UK needs a museum of colonialism, says historian William Dalrymple", *theguardian.com*, 16.09.2020, https://www.theguardian.com/books/2020/sep/16/uk-needs-a-museum-of-colonialism-says-historian-william-dalrymple (accessed 11.10.2021), Copyright Guardian News & Media Ltd 2021; **pp. 14–16**: Yesufu, Aisha. "The Nigeria That I See". *Remaking Nigeria. Sixty Years, Sixty Voices.*, edited by Chido Onumah, Premium Times Books, 2020, pp. 44–49; **p. 19**: Lo Wei Wei, Miriam. "Bumboat Cruise on the Singapore River." Westerly 50, Westerly Magazine, 2005, pp. 87–88; **pp. 20–22**: "Digitaler Stadtstaat: Wie Singapur zur Smart Nation wurde", *FAZ*, 31.05.2021, Christoph Hein © Alle Rechte vorbehalten. Frankfurter Allgemeine Zeitung GmbH, Frankfurt. Zur Verfügung gestellt vom Frankfurter Allgemeine Archiv; **pp. 24–26**: Rolston, Bill. "Democratic disruption. Ireland's colonial hangover." LSE, 5 Jul. 2019, blogs.lse.ac.uk/wps/2019/07/05/ democratic-disruption-irelands-colonial-hangover (accessed 8.10. 2021); **p. 24** Quote by Michael D. Higgins: Higgins, Michael D. "Irish President Michael D Higgins's toast at the Queen's state banquet: In full." *Belfast Telegraph*, 8 Apr. 2014. Accessed 16 December 2021; **p. 27**: Quote by Higgins, Michael D. "Empire shaped Ireland's past. A century after partition, it still shapes our present." *theguardian.com*, 11 Feb. 2021, www.theguardian.com/commentisfree/2021/feb/11/empire-ireland-century-partition-present-britain-history (accessed 8.10.2021)

Song

p. 23: *Forty Shades of Green*. Copyright Warner Chappell Music GmbH & Co. KG Germany/Text, (OT) Cash, Johnny